Rhetoric

of

Logos

A Primer
for
Visual
Language

niggli

Eduard Helmann
Brian Switzer (Ed.)

"The arts were born of *Chance* and *Observation*, fostered by *Use* and *Experiment*, and matured by *Knowledge* and *Reason*."

LEON BATTISTA ALBERTI

Contents

Foreword

Establishing new ideas in any field takes perseverance and patience. Design, and particularly graphic design or visual communication, is resistant to the introduction of theories to guide its practice. Theory somehow threatens to dispel the nimbus of the designer as a genius, unhorsing him from his award-armored steed gathered to defend his talents. Yet design and graphic designers need theories to better understand their field and their value to society. That need makes this introduction to the "rhetoric of logos" especially valuable. It will enable professionals to better understand existing marks and use the principles of rhetoric to create new marks or logos.

As Eduard Helmann says himself, he is standing on the shoulders of giants. The seed for this publication was planted and carefully nourished in Constance by the late Professor Michele Baviera (for inspiring and guiding Helmann's love of logos), Professor Dr. Volker Friedrich (for seeing and teaching the value of rhetoric for design) and in some small ways by myself (by believing in him and in seeing the value of his work). Thanks are in order to NIGGLI for publishing the book, as well as the UNIVERSITY OF APPLIED SCIENCES, CONSTANCE, who provided a substantial portion of the funding. As a teacher, it is always a great pleasure for me to see my students succeed. It is my desire that this work will be read and used by young designers (and teachers) looking for guidance in a world overfilled with visual input.

Professor Brian Switzer

———————————————

Abstract

Communication design is at a loss for words! Lost for words in the sense that it lacks the specialized vocabulary to describe causal relationships. The little terminology that does exist is very vague. This vagueness, which results in a lack of reasoning, is based on an imbalance of theory and practice.

A scientific basis is needed to establish a specific terminology and develop a language for communication design. Luckily, this terminology and language do not have to be created since they already exist. What is actually needed is to follow Bernard of Chartres's metaphor and stand on the shoulders of the giants to benefit from the pioneering efforts of the past. In this case the giant is rhetoric with its extensive vocabulary that can be adopted by communication design.

This book analyzes logos in terms of *rhetorical devices*. The aim is to discover the role of *rhetorical devices* in logos and deduce a system for logo design. This is followed by the description of a method of analysis that can be used to examine the effects and *modes of persuasion—logos, ethos,* and *pathos*—of logos. The final outcome is a descriptive model that offers designers practical guidelines for systematic and structured working.

Collect, compare, sort, and gain insight

"He who loves practice without theory is like the sailor
who boards ship without a rudder and compass and never
knows where he may cast." LEONARDO DA VINCI

Communication design has always been and remains primarily practice-based. In the 1960s there were some attempts, especially by the HFG ULM, to establish a scientific basis for design, but
with limited success. Only recently has the design sector once again
attempted to create a theoretical basis for the discipline. The lack of
a theory is especially conspicuous when communication designers try
to precisely verbalize the purpose and benefits of their work. This is
due in part to inadequacy of the terminology required to describe the
design process, and is also due to the absence of an established method
for analyzing the intended effects of designed artifacts.

However, the knowledge and methods of other sciences
can be used to develop a theoretical foundation. For example biology,
where plants, animals and organisms have been systematically collected, sorted, juxtaposed and compared over a long period of time
to discover key insights. Each plant, animal and living organism is

categorized and allocated a fixed place in a system. They could thus be put in relation to each other and statements could be made regarding their mutual relationships, similarities and differences—statements about the identity of the individual objects. This book applies a similar approach while trying to answer the following questions:

> How can the terminology of rhetoric be applied to communication design, more specifically corporate design?
> How does this affect communication design?
> Can the terms be used to derive methods that can assist designers in analysis, creation and argumentation?
> How can this reduce the complexity of work processes?

To find answers to these questions, the first chapter of this primer briefly describes the history of logos and explains how corporate design has evolved since its inception. In addition, the five elements of corporate design and their effects are explained. Chapter B discusses the terminology of rhetoric and describes previous work and findings of design rhetoric. Furthermore it provides a catalog of 16 *rhetorical devices* including instructions for their application.

Chapter C introduces a method of analysis that examines logos in terms of their intended formal-esthetic and communicative effects.

Before we embark on this journey to the past, one needs to understand the terminology used in this book. The term logo is derived from the Greek *logos*, which means "word" or "speech". In the strict sense of the word it actually only denotes the word mark. The more precise term to use for the entire concept would be mark. However, logo is the more commonly used term, which is why it is used to talk about the general concept. In places where the word mark or figurative mark are explicitly stated, the respective term is used. In addition, the book distinguishes between *stylistic devices* and *rhetorical devices*. *Stylistic devices* include color, shape and typography, while *rhetorical devices* refer to the content-related tools that are the main focus of this book.

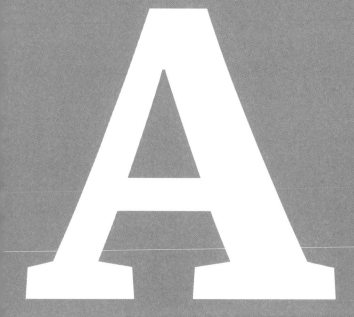

A—I
Going back to the roots—
The origins of logos

What we today generally describe as a logo has a very long history, dating back approximately 5,000 years. First indications of the use of early logos were found by scientists in ancient Egyptian tombs. They discovered hieroglyphs that showed domesticated animals carrying specific brands.[1] Later on, Roman embossed stamps were found that were used for labeling oil lamps.[2]

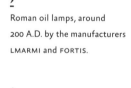

> [2]
> Roman oil lamps, around
> 200 A.D. by the manufacturers
> LMARMI and FORTIS.

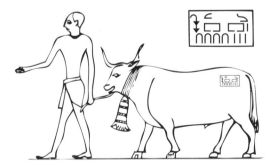

[1]
Egyptian tombstone with a
brand mark on the ox, around
1900 B.C.

Heraldry

The heralds, who can rightfully be described as the founders of today's corporate design, were public officials with expertise in coats of arms. They were in charge of the "visual image" of knights during tournaments. They kept written records of which coat of arms was used by whom and developed a system for the differentiation of coats of arms. [3] The rules for this were based on the basic form of the shield. Initially, they involved only simple divisions and geometrical elements. Later on, more elaborate lines, colors, depictions of people, plants, animals, etc. were added. [4]

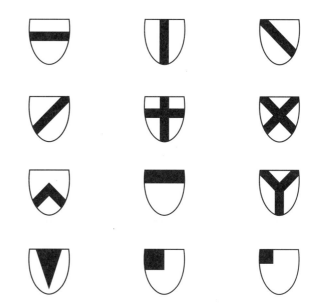

> **≥**
>
> The coats of arms were originally founded on basic elements. From left to right, top to bottom: fess, pale, bend, bend sinister, cross, saltire, chevron, chief, pall, pile, quarter, canton.

A — I

Guilds' coats of arms

The privilege of owning a coat of arms was originally reserved to members of nobility. Each trade received its own coat of arms and the artisans were obligated to attach these coats of arms to their workshops—the aim was to identify the quality and origins of the goods to protect citizens from fraud. [5]

›

Identification of different guilds by emblems, from left to right, top to bottom: Cobblers, fishermen, butchers, clothiers, weavers, painters, millers, brick masons, carpenters, roofers, tailors, bakers, saddlers, blacksmiths, furriers, tanners.

*Industrialization
and branding*

Industrialization and the resulting mass production led to increased economic competition. Branding evolved and became a key component of corporate culture. In 1963, the business economist Konrad Mellerowicz coined the definition of the term brand, which is still in use today for the characterization of branded items, as follows:

"Branded items are ready-made goods that are created for private use and that are available in an extended sales area with a special defining feature (brand) that signifies their origin in a uniform style, equal quantity and in constant or improved quality. These characteristics along with the advertising that promotes the items allowed them to gain the acceptance of the involved business communities (consumers, dealers and manufacturers) (secondary meaning)."[6]

Mellerowicz thus established the classical concept of branding.[7] This was soon followed by additional terms for brands.

>
Manufacturers brands from
around 1900: AEG, BAYER
and DR. OETKER.

A — I

Branding

From 1950 to 1960, the level of competition in the Federal Republic of Germany was stable. Classical manufacturer brands dominated the market and the aim was to establish a strong brand personality.[8] Retail brands entered the market in the mid 1960s. This resulted in a conflict between manufacturers and retailers. Manufacturers had two options to cope with this: either to cooperate or to push the retailers out of the market.[9]

In the 1980s, consumer behavior became even more dynamic. The market became more differentiated and polarized. As a result, budget and luxury brands were established. Service brands developed at the same time.[10]

In the 1990s, technology companies realized that their products did not market themselves, which led to the development of industrial brands.[11]

Today, even cities and regions regard themselves as business-oriented service providers. They apply the prevalent practice of branding and have introduced city and regional brands.[12]

Classic

‹
Retail brands:
JA! and K-CLASSIC.

›
Luxury brand: MAYBACH.
Budget brand: DACIA.

MAYBACH

There are various reasons for the emergence of these many types of branding. However, branding always aims to accomplish three goals—ensuring the origins, belonging to a social community, and clarifying ownership. [13]

The various types of branding are at first confusing, nevertheless, the definitions are useful for the positioning of brands, especially for "brand creators". This is because each brand term describes specific characteristics that are essential for the development of a brand.

In the next section we will look at the history of corporate design, from its early days when it was still known as the design program, via corporate identity, to brand identity.

<

Service brands:

DEUTSCHE BANK and TUI.

SIEMENS

>

Industrial goods brands:

SIEMENS and

ASEA BROWN BOVERI.

>

Region brand: SÜDTIROL.

City brand: DÜSSELDORF

[1] Cf. Mollerup, P., 2013, 27

[2] Ibid., 32

[3] Ibid., 17

[4] Ibid., 20

[5] Cf. Hamann, S., 2007, 42

[6] Cf. Mellerowicz, K., 1963, 39

[7] Cf. Bruhn, M., 2001, 15

[8] Cf. Meffert, H., Bruhn, M., 1984, 10f.

[9] Cf. Bruhn, M., 2001, 20

[10] Ibid., 20

[11] Ibid., 21

[12] Ibid., 22

[13] Cf. Mollerup, P., 2013, 27

Design programs—
Corporate identity—
Brand identity

Design programs

Historically speaking, the concept of corporate identity is closely linked with the history of design. Both, in turn, only evolved due to the industrial revolution.[1] In the period from 1907–1914, Peter Behrens, a pioneer of design programs, developed for the AEG company buildings, exhibition spaces, workers residences, advertising materials and electrical household appliances—i.e. the entire visual image of the company. Behrens, who was an architect, graphic designer, industrial designer, and painter, was probably one of the first pioneers to realize that a systematic design program was of particular benefit to large corporations.[2]

In the 1930s other companies followed suit, such as CONTAINER CORPORATION OF AMERICA and in the 1950s IBM with Paul Rand as its designer.[3] In 1961, LUFTHANSA, whose image was developed by Hans Conrad together with Otl Aicher, and KLM, who employed FHK Henrion as designer, also adopted this approach.[4] This comprehensive system of a uniform design for a company came to be known as design programs. Based on the corporate attitude, the designers developed an authentic and uniform image that incorporated all areas of a company—architecture, transport

A—II   vehicles, uniforms, advertising, and product packaging. It was an important management tool at that time. In the 1970s, other areas, such as marketing, fueled the concept with their own approaches. This resulted in a comprehensive approach that is today known as corporate identity.

Corporate identity   Design programs, a term that was originally coined by design, became outdated no later than in 1980 with the publication of the book "Corporate Identity: Grundlagen, Funktionen, Fallbeispiele" (Corporate identity: basics, functions, case studies) by Birkigt, Stadler and Funck. The authors aimed to establish a scientific framework for corporate identities. One of their major achievements to this day is the separation of corporate identity and corporate image.[5] The authors described the difference as follows: "Corporate identity describes the internal image of a company, while the corporate image is its external image. That means that the corporate image is the projection of the identity to the social realm."[6] Another achievement was the subdivision of corporate identity into the areas of behavior, appearance and communications, with corporate behavior as the most important of the three.[7] The authors described the separation of image and communication as follows: "If the formulation of the image is treated as an independent company presentation, while the development of the company has long since taken a different approach and has found a new identity, then a traditionally maintained image becomes a ball and chain that can cause schizophrenia in the corporate identity."[8] Regarding the causes for the separation of actual development from communication, the authors state that: "Tactically applied corporate communication often focuses, frequently quite necessarily so, more on the occasion and on addressing current target groups than on the true-to-concept depiction of the corporate identity. To achieve maximum results, in such cases the focus can easily turn more to the man on the street (= target group) than on the bible of corporate identity. [...] The synergy effect of consistently identity-oriented communication is eliminated in this case and if this deviating behavior continues, it can significantly disrupt the efforts of constructing or maintaining a corporate identity. This often results in schizophrenic corporate communication [...]."[9]

This leads to the question of whether this strict segregation of corporate identity and corporate image is absolutely necessary. Heinz Kroehl, an author who also studied corporate identities in depth, doubts this, and fully incorporates communicative behavior and design in his model.[10] Kroehl states that the development of corporate identities did not evolve beyond the stage described by Birkigt, Stadler and Funck.[11] For this to change, he postulated that findings from various sciences such as business management, sociology, psychology, communications, and design must be merged, and Kroehl saw the biggest theoretical deficiencies in the latter.[12] In recent years, another term became essential to the sector—brand identity, which will be explained below.

A—II

Brand identity

Corporate identity creates the identity of a company, while branding, which originates in modern marketing theory, is used as a tool for providing products with an identity. [13] The term branding is nowadays also used on company level, but this use is currently heavily debated. Nevertheless, it can be expected to prevail. Evidence for this can be found in "Marks of Excellence" by Per Mollerup. In the first edition, the book still differentiated clearly between design programs and branding, in the new updated edition, the term brand identity is used exclusively. [14] Therefore, branding is used to develop and maintain a brand. The term brand refers to products, services, companies, organizations, events, or locations. It consists of a brand essence, the presence of the brand on the market, and the image resulting thereof. [15]

Design as the original developer and impulse generator has lost its former preeminence. One possible reason may be its lack of a scientific basis. In this regard, marketing dominates the sector because it actually creates a foundation and makes it public. According to Kroehl, the developments regarding corporate identities are not sufficient. In his opinion, design has only limited or no basic principles. This is why it is important that designers are also involved in interdisciplinary approaches.

[1] Cf. Kroehl, H., 2000, 23

[2] Cf. Schneider, B., 2009, 50

[3] Ibid., 131

[4] Cf. Schaughnessy, A., 2013, 92–98

[5] Cf. Birkigt, K., Stadler, M., et. al., 2002, 23

[6] Birkigt, K., Stadler, M., et. al., 2002, 23

[7] Cf. Birkigt, K., Stadler, M., et. al., 2002, 20

[8] Birkigt, K., Stadler, M., et. al., 2002, 21

[9] Birkigt, K., Stadler, M., et. al., 2002, 21f.

[10] Cf. Kroehl, H., 2000, 19

[11] Cf. Kroehl, H., 2000, 56

[12] Ibid., 17

[13] Cf. Mollerup, P., 1997, 45

[14] Cf. Mollerup, P., 1997, 46 and 2013, 45

[15] Cf. Mollerup, P., 2013, 46

Five elements—
The elements of corporate design

───────────

Corporate design consists of five elements: logo, typography, color, layout grid/shape, and image style. The weight of each variable differs from one designer to another. For example, to Erik Spiekermann, the typography and color are key components of an image.[1]

A successful corporate image, however, can only be accomplished through the interplay of all elements that have to be matched to each other. To understand the advantages and disadvantages of each, it is worthwhile to examine the elements individually.

A—III

Grid and shape

Initially, we must differentiate between the layout grid and the shape. The layout grid is the invisible component whose purpose is to structure the shape. Shapes can "carry, separate, connect, arbitrate, calm, distinguish and organize."[2] In corporate design shape is the element that is the most difficult to categorize, as everything that is designed ultimately constitutes a shape. Intelligently applied, the shape has narrative qualities that ensure recognition.[3]

︿

Once the shape has been firmly established in the mind, brand recognition requires no further elements.

‹

The curved line of COCA-COLA ensures brand recognition and is a prominent element in the overall image.

	When evaluating typography for example,
Typography	one must differentiate between its application and character. If a particularly large font size is used, e.g. in headlines, it naturally gains

more attention than a smaller one.

Type is the element with the greatest presence in corporate design, because it conveys information—generally speaking, we receive information by reading.[4] The capacity of non-experts to distinguish among fonts is very limited. Nevertheless, it is immediately noticeable to everyone if, for example, MERCEDES-BENZ is written in another typeface.

Another characteristic of fonts are the associations they create. Capitals are associated with power and Fraktur fonts have been erroneously allocated to National Socialism. Consistently applied, as practiced by DEUTSCHE BAHN, MERCEDES-BENZ or BOSCH, the font plays a major role in identification.

>

AUDI claim in the corporate
font of MERCEDES-BENZ
(Corporate A).

Truth in Engineering

The best or nothing.

<

MERCEDES-BENZ claim in
the corporate font of AUDI
(AudiType).

A—III

Color

In the hierarchy of perception, color takes the top spot. Clearly distinguished colors can be readily allocated to specific organizations (DEUTSCHE POST, MILKA, TELEKOM, NIVEA). Even from a distance they symbolize the company within a fracture of a second. This is why color is very important when it comes to recognition.

When developing an image, two strategies can be applied. One of them is to associate color with meaning. However, this can be difficult as color perception is subjective and people can have specific (and thus different) associations with colors. The second strategy is the deliberate selection of a unique color to distinguish the company from its competition. Mathias Beyrow describes color as the most effective component of corporate design, however, without providing concrete evidence. [5]

›
Corporate colors as a
tool for recognition of
companies. From top
to bottom: DEUTSCHE
POST, MILKA, TELEKOM
and NIVEA.

Image style
The image seems to be the most suitable element to generate emotions. However, this effect is short-lived and the rate of wear that is caused by today's flood of images leads to a loss of attention to images. If images are applied consistently, however, they can aid orientation. The world of images used by the DEUTSCHE BAHN consistently highlights the horizontal view, lending consistency to the corporate image. Another example is the world of images of O_2. It has been deeply ingrained in our consciousness and as a result, the image can be associated with the company without any text at all.

>
The distinct images of O_2 enable the observer to allocate this image to the company without further information.

A—III

Logo

The logo is possibly the most important element when it comes to identification. Uli Mayer-Johanson, co-founder of META DESIGN, said that "anyone who has worked with companies on the identity-based further development of their own brand knows that for the employees the identity of the company is symbolized by the logo to a much stronger degree than any of the other components of corporate design."[6] Anton Stankowski described the logo as a "visual hook, signal, and identification mark at the same time. [...] The company identifies itself through its logo."[7] For Beyrow also, the logo is "the most powerful element in the repertoire of companies."[8]

Nevertheless, a frequent error of companies is to solely rely on the logo as the only element of recognition.[9] Moreover, one should not expect too much of a logo, as it can rarely convey an "image, mind set, cohesive identity, easy recognition, and significance" all at once.[10] This is why Gert Mayr-Keber does not consider logos to be very important when it comes to identification. At the same time, he notes that as a constant element and unchanging image bearer it is a fixed point of reference.[11]

Google

SAMSUNG

<

The ten most successful corporations (the 100 best global brands 2015, interbrand) and their logos. From left to right, top to bottom: APPLE, GOOGLE, COCA-COLA, MICROSOFT, IBM, TOYOTA, SAMSUNG, GENERAL ELECTRIC, MCDONALD'S, AMAZON.

A—III What distinguishes a successful logo? There is no general answer to this question. On the one hand, companies have different strategic goals for using logos. On the other hand, there are no specific analysis tools to examine intended visual effects and communicative persuasion tools. Yet such an analysis would allow the identification of the individual phenomena and thus make them explicable to outsiders. The terminology and methods of rhetoric, described in the following chapter, are well suited for this purpose.

[1] Cf. Spiekerman, E., 2013, 138 – 150

[2] Beyrow, M., 2013, 263

[3] Ibid., 263

[4] Cf. Beyrow, M., 2013, 138

[5] Cf. Beyrow, M., 2013, 265f.

[6] Wiedmann, J., 2009, 8

[7] Cf. Birkigt, K., Stadler, M., et. al., 2002, 203

[8] Cf. Beyrow, M., 2013, 267

[9] Cf. Birkigt, K., Stadler, M., et. al., 2002, 294

[10] Ibid.

[11] Ibid.

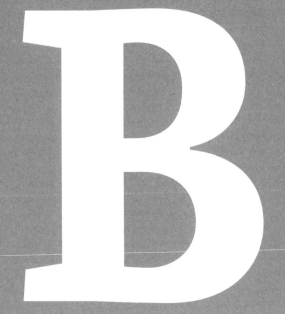

B — I   *Marking and leaving an impression*

The logo serves as a distinctive mark and ambassador at the same time. It creates an identity, causes attention and distinction, it informs, provides orientation, inspires, and wants to be remembered. In addition, it provides information about the personality of the company, appeals to the observer, argues, and wants to gain support for the company as its representative. It also wants to affect the behavior, attitude and opinion of the receiver.

The question is how and by what means does it accomplish all these tasks. And how designers and companies can apply this knowledge. The answer can be found by looking at the individual elements and clarifying their position in the overall picture. The individual elements are the visual *stylistic devices* and the visual *rhetorical devices*. Visual *rhetorical devices* are identified by examining the stages of the speech production process and *modes of persuasion of speeches*. The aim of the following explanation is to introduce the reader to rhetorical terms.

Classical rhetoric

Also known as the art of discourse, or the study of oration; Greek *rhētoriké téchnē*; Latin *rhetorica, ars rhetorika, ars bene dicendi.* In the German encyclopedia Brockhaus, rhetoric is defined as the art of effective speaking. For more than 2,500 years the theory and practical application of rhetoric has been focused on human communication. For this purpose, principles, methods, and tools were developed that are both suited for the analysis and creation of speeches.[1] The main aim is to make the speaker's subjective opinion on a matter publically acceptable.[2] This is why Aristotle described it as "[...] the given ability of recognizing the persuasive in any subject."[3] This shows that rhetoric is mainly a cognitive science.

Production process of a speech

The *production process of a speech* is one of the key instruments of rhetoric. Consisting of five stages, it provides orators with systematic instructions. In the first stage, *inventio* (invention), the subject of the speech is determined and the required material is collected. For this purpose, the speaker can resort to specific tools *(topos)* that facilitate the search for arguments, proof, and evidence. In the second step, *dispositio* (disposition), the subject of

B — II   the speech is arranged and organized. Arguments are weighed, sorted according to their relevance and subsequently allocated to the four parts of the speech (introduction, presentation of facts, argumentation, and conclusion).

In the third step, *elocutio* (elocution), the speech is drafted. Aspects such as correctness, clearness, appropriateness, and precision are the top criteria. The speaker can resort to a comprehensive catalog of *rhetorical devices* that can be used to influence the tone of the speech and the argumentation process. The fourth stage, *memoria* (memory), is about memorizing the speech. Speakers can learn various mnemonic devices. The fifth and final step, *actio* (delivery), deals with the public presentation. The focus is on gestures, facial expression and voice of the speaker, which, when used skillfully, can help persuade the audience.[4]

Modes of persuasion   To convince their audience of their points of view, orators can utilize three *modes of persuasion—logos, ethos,* and *pathos.*[5] With their help, and the *rhetorical devices* allocated to them, speakers can examine the appropriateness of their speeches. Below are brief descriptions of the three *modes of persuasion* followed by a more detailed explanation.

› Speakers can argue logically and objectively present the facts *(logos).*
› They can apply persuasive means that present evidence regarding their character to establish their credibility *(ethos).*

› They can apply persuasive means that appeal to the audience's emotions *(pathos)*. [6]

Reason and instruction (logos) Speakers must present their cause rationally or else they risk losing their credibility. Yet a factually presented speech does not have to be free of emotions. If the arguments are logical and convincing and the cause is presented vividly, speakers can count on the trust and approval of the audience. [7] However, if the presentation is too factual there is the danger of the audience becoming bored and not paying attention to the speaker. [8] The suitable style for this case is factual and plain *(genus humile)* clearly stating logical conclusions and presenting the facts openly. [9]

Pleasure and entertainment (ethos) By describing their own character, speakers gain the audience's sympathy. If the audience feels that the statements of the speaker are in line with its own ideals, the result is agreement and good will. [10] The perception is not limited to speech but also to the demeanor, the clothing and behavior—i.e. the entire appearance of the speaker. [11] The suitable expressive style here is the middle style *(genus medium)*. The speaker rarely resorts to *tropes* and *schemes* as the aim is to create a natural impression. By avoiding extremes, the style creates a bond, refreshes the attention, and prevents monotony. [12]

B — II   *Appealing to emotions (pathos)*   While *ethos* is considered
to be mildly appealing to emotions, *pathos* is distinguished by causing
intense, immediate and transient emotions. [13] Passion is primarily
caused by the speaker actually living out the emotion and being
capable of expressing it. [14] The powerful emotional appeals not only
intend to convince the audience to adopt the opinion and purpose
of the speaker, but the hearers should literally be swept away by the
passion of the speaker. [15] The high style *(genus grande)* is used here.
Tropes and *schemes* are used excessively in this style. [16]

Stylistics

Another major sector of rhetoric is the study
of *rhetorical devices* that are described in the
elocutio. The term *rhetorical device* denotes the
deliberate deviation from the literal meaning
of words. During classical antiquity it was noted that there is a difference between what is said and how it is said. [17] To allow orators to
proceed systematically, *rhetorical devices* were classified and systematically organized. In general, they can be divided into *tropes, schemes,*
and *figures of thought.* [18] The three categories each affect the tone of
the speech as well as the argumentative process and will be described
in greater detail below.

 Tropes, also known as *figures of substitution* or *circumscription,* are distinguished by their deliberate departure from the common use. For example: "With this, he handed Socrates the cup."
(Platon) instead of "With this he handed Socrates the poison."

Tropes have different effects on the audience. They make facts more vivid, precise, exciting, or varied.[19]

The function of *schemes* is the illustration, clarification, or embellishment of a thought—in some instances they can also affect the meaning of what is said, similar to *tropes*. They change the normal arrangement of words and sentence parts,[20] for example "But O dear, O dear, O deary, When the end comes sad and dreary!" (W. Busch), or "I do not live to eat, but eat to live" (Quintilian). The change is by addition, omission, or rearrangement of individual words, groups of words, or parts of sentences.[21]

Figures of thought organize the aims and objectives of the speaker in larger contexts. They are used to control the argumentation, to advance it or to extend it or to sharpen ideas.[22]

[1] Cf. Brockhaus, 1996, 345

[2] Cf. Ueding, G., Steinbrink, B., 2011, 1

[3] Aristotle, 1999, 11

[4] Cf. Brockhaus, 1996, 345f.

[5] Cf. Ueding, G., Steinbrink, B., 2011, 278

[6] Cf. Ottmers, C., 2007, 123

[7] Cf. Ueding, G., Steinbrink, B., 2011, 280

[8] Ibid.

[9] Ibid.

[10] Cf. Ueding, G., Steinbrink, B., 2011, 281

[11] Ibid.

[12] Ibid.

[13] Cf. Kraus, M., 2003, 690

[14] Cf. Ueding, G., Steinbrink, B., 2011, 282

[15] Cf. Ottmers, C., 2007, 127f.

[16] Cf. Ueding, G., Steinbrink, B., 2011, 282

[17] Cf. Ehses, H., 2008, 116

[18] Cf. Göttert, K. H., 1991, 47

[19] Cf. Ottmers, C., 2007, 171f.

[20] Ibid., 164

[21] Cf. Ueding, G., Steinbrink, B., 2011, 302

[22] Cf. Ottmers, C., 2007, 188

The association—
Design and classical rhetoric

Leon Battista Alberti already proved in the 15th century that rhetoric can also be applied to other sectors. Contrary to its original purpose, he applied it to architecture, painting and music.[1] Since the mid-20th century there have also been some attempts to use the knowledge of rhetoric in design. Gui Bonsiepe already showed in the mid-1960s that advertising messages can be analyzed using verbal *rhetorical devices*. He applied the vocabulary of the verbal stylistics to the area of visual communication.[2] More than 20 years later, in the 1980s, Hanno Ehses and Ellen Lupton[3] studied *rhetorical devices* and their application to logos. Both Bonsiepe and Ehses recognized the advantages of this association. This knowledge, according to Ehses, allows designers to deliberately choose specific means, especially during brainstorming, and to implement their ideas in a visual form.[4] They also realized that even though communication designers may use *rhetorical devices* in their daily work, they rarely do so consciously. However, their insights and the benefits of their research did not receive much acclaim from practitioners. Only in the past few years, Arne Scheuermann, Gesche Joost[5] and Volker Friedrich[6] have been attempting to retrieve this treasure trove of information.

B — III   Another example for the application of rhetoric in design
is the *relevance model* by Matthias Beyrow that can be found in the
"Kompendium für Corporate Identity & Design" (Corporate identity &
design compendium). According to Beyrow, the model is based on the
concept of visual rhetoric. He aimed to discover the structures and
patterns of logos to categorize them according to their *appeal strategy*.

The *relevance model* divides logos into three categories:
› Logos that create a *presence*. The designer uses formal means to
  capture the attention of the target group.
› Logos that convey *substance*. The logo presents values or unique
  selling points of the company.
› Logos that convey *references*. Cultural or historically already
  established characteristics of other areas are visualized. [7]

These three categories do not act in isolation, instead
they intersect and overlap. For example, logos that convey *substance*
and/or *reference* can create *presence* at the same time. This categorization therefore indicates which strategies and approaches are
utilized by the individual logos to convey information about their
sender. Thus, logos can be divided according to their context-related
aspects. [8] However, the question of which devices can be used to
achieve the above-mentioned goals remains unanswered.

Logos that create a
presence: BEST, TEMPO,
LUDWIG-MAXIMILIANS-
UNIVERSITÄT.

Logos that convey
substance: WOOLMARK,
NATURKUNDE MUSEUM
BERLIN, HAUSHAHN.

Logos that are based
on *references*:
UPS, C&A, ROLEX.

B — III   The analysis is based on this and other research and deals
with the question of the role played by *rhetorical devices* in logos. Are
they what Ehses describes as the "idea"? And if yes, do they relate
more to the contextual or the formal idea? Can they even be used to
systematically search for ideas? The ultimate aim is to discover and
develop patterns and rules that can be applied to analysis on the one
hand and to the design process on the other.

[1] Cf. Ehses, H., 2008, 112

[2] Cf. Bonsieppe, G., 2008, 27

[3] Cf. Ehses, H., Lupton, E., 1988, 16ff.

[4] Ehses, H., 2008, 116f.

[5] Joost, G., Scheuermann, A., 2008

[6] Friedrich, V., www.designrhetorik.de

[7] Cf. Beyrow, M., 2013, 268f.

[8] Ibid.

B — IV   *Analysis and classification*

As described in the previous section, there are three types of *rhetorical devices: tropes, schemes* and *figures of thought.* The latter are used by the speaker to structure large textual associations. As logos are for the most part reduced to a single statement, they rarely contain *figures of thought* and these are therefore not included in the following analysis of logos. Among *tropes,* we shall look at *metaphor, metonymy, synecdoche, onomatopoeia, emphasis, euphemism,* and *hyperbole.* The *schemes* are divided into three categories: *schemes of addition, of transposition* and *omission.* The analyzed *schemes of addition* include *alliteration, anaphora, polyptoton, diaphora, climax* and *anticlimax;* while *anastrophe* and *parenthesis* are analyzed as *schemes of transposition* and *ellipsis* as a *scheme of omission.* [1]

This analysis does not claim to be comprehensive. Additional devices can be continuously added to enhance the categorization.

Procedure

The *rhetorical devices* are initially presented based on their definition in the theory of rhetoric and explained using examples. They are then abstracted for their visual use and allocated to the respective context. In conclusion, their interrelation is examined. [2] The main criteria for choosing the presented logos is the definitive identification of the contained *rhetorical device* and their general level of recognition.

Rhetorical devices

A ⟶ B **Tropes—figures of circumscription**

A + A + A **Schemes—figures of addition**

C A B **Schemes—figures of transposition**

Ɩ **Schemes—figures of omission**

B — IV

$$A \xrightarrow{\text{A1}} 1$$

Metaphor

The literal translation of the Greek word *metaphérein* means to "carry/transfer elsewhere". In Latin, *Metaphora* means "carrying over a meaning". This translation already indicates the nature of the *metaphor*—it is the comparison of two terms that are not factually related to each other to create a new meaning. For this to take place there must be some associative similarity between the two terms. However, this association cannot be precisely defined as it depends on the subjective opinion, experience, and individual associative capacity of the recipient. [3] The classical example of a *metaphor* is the sentence "He is a <u>lion</u> [in battle]" (Inst.or. VIII.6.9). The actually intended term, such as a "courageous fighter", is replaced by the term "lion" and thus the characteristics that are historically and culturally conventionally connected to this term, such as courage, power, and strength, are associated with the described person. [4]

The *metaphor*, therefore, consists of three parts. (A) The intended meaning or *tenor*, (1) what is actually said or *vehicle*, and (A1) the point of comparison, which creates an analogy between (A) and (1). Substituting the *tenor* with the *vehicle* puts what is being said in a new, formerly unknown light. This may also involve added information. *Metaphors* are associated with two functional effects.

B — IV   A purely ornamental function that makes the fact appear in a more favorable light, and a conceptual function that expands the point of view and provides new insights. [5]

Abstraction

Metaphors are used in word marks or figurative marks to associate specific characteristics with a company. For example, the figurative mark of LUFTHANSA associates the characteristics of the crane with the airline. These characteristics can be derived from various sources. In heraldry, for example, the crane is a symbol of caution and sleepless watchfulness. [6] Thus, the figurative mark becomes a *metaphor* for safe flying. The observer who deciphers this message recognizes the common characteristics and draws conclusions regarding safe flying. However, for those who do not decipher the intended meaning, the crane remains an arbitrary image. This is why it is important to precisely identify the similarities between the *tenor* and the *vehicle* and to make sure that the target group is capable of deciphering the message.

Lufthansa

A The figurative mark of LUFT-
HANSA features a crane—in
heraldry a symbol of caution
and sleepless watchfulness.

B — IV *Metaphors* are used in figurative and word marks. When a *metaphor* is used in both, the designer must decide whether this is expedient or redundant. The decision depends on two factors: the target group and the desired emphasis of additional characteristics of the company. For example, the logo of the logistics company HERMES uses a *metaphor* in both the word and figurative mark. The association with Hermes, the Greek messenger of the gods, is created by both the word mark as well as the depiction of a wing in the figurative mark. As the company addresses a wide target group, this repetition is warranted, perhaps even necessary.

The French luxury brand HERMÈS handles this *rhetorical device* in a different way. In this case, the *metaphor* is in the word mark and most likely indicates Hermes as well, however, this time in his function as the patron god of merchants. The figurative mark, however, featuring a horse, carriage and a man wearing a top hat is a reference to the beginnings of the manufacturer who originally produced high quality leather saddles. Therefore, HERMÈS makes two statements at once: safety and tradition.

A

B

A Both the word mark and the figurative mark of the logistics company symbolize Hermes the Greek messenger of the gods. This is a mythological *metaphor*.

B HERMÈS uses the mythological *metaphor* in the word mark, while the figurative mark contains a *metonymy* (page 64).

B — IV

Classes of metaphors

Metaphors have different bases that can be described as classes. Heinrich Plett divides them into the following main categories: *nature metaphors, color metaphors, mineralogical metaphors, cosmological metaphors, body part metaphors* and *nautical metaphors.*[2] When it comes to logos, this categorization can be complemented by *mythological metaphors* and *object metaphors.* One example of a *mythological metaphor* is the logo of the sports equipment manufacturer NIKE. An example of an *object metaphor* is the logo of CITI BANK.

As all these categories consist of general terms, they can be subdivided further. *Nature metaphors* can additionally be divided into *meteorological metaphors* and *animal metaphors,* which in turn can be subdivided into mammals, birds, reptiles, amphibians, etc.

A The figurative mark of ING-DIBA contains a *nature metaphor*.

B The word mark of the environmental protection organization GREENPEACE uses a *color metaphor*.

C The logo of LINCOLN contains a diamond—a *mineralogical metaphor*.

D The electronic stores chain SATURN uses the planet of the same name in both its word and figurative marks—*cosmological metaphor*.

E A *body part metaphor*, the head of an Indian, is contained in the logo of ŠKODA.

F The logo of automobile manufacturer ROVER contains a *nautical metaphor*.

G The sword of Nike, the goddess of victory, is also the logo of the sports equipment manufacturer NIKE—a *mythological metaphor*.

H The umbrella as a *metaphor* for protection in the logo of CITI BANK—an *object metaphor*.

A1 The *meteorological metaphor* —a subdivision of the *nature metaphor*—is found in the OPEL logo.

A2 Subdivisions of the *nature metaphor* into bird, reptile, and amphibian are used by the publishing house PENGUIN, the clothing company LACOSTE and FROG DESIGN, a product design agency.

B — IV

Encoding the
metaphor

The recognition depends on the connection, or the closeness or distance of the substituted terms. If there is a direct connection, i.e. (A) is replaced by (B), we talk about a direct *metaphor*. If the connection is indirect, for example from (A) to (K), it is an implied *metaphor*.[8] A direct connection from (A) to (B) can be found in APPLE'S first logo. It shows Newton sitting under a tree— an insinuation of the discovery of gravity. Computer technology is thus associated with science. The current figurative mark with a single "byte" missing from an apple is a good example of an *implied metaphor*. This is because an apple missing a bite has little to do with a computer manufacturer. Instead, it triggers association with concepts including the history of creation.

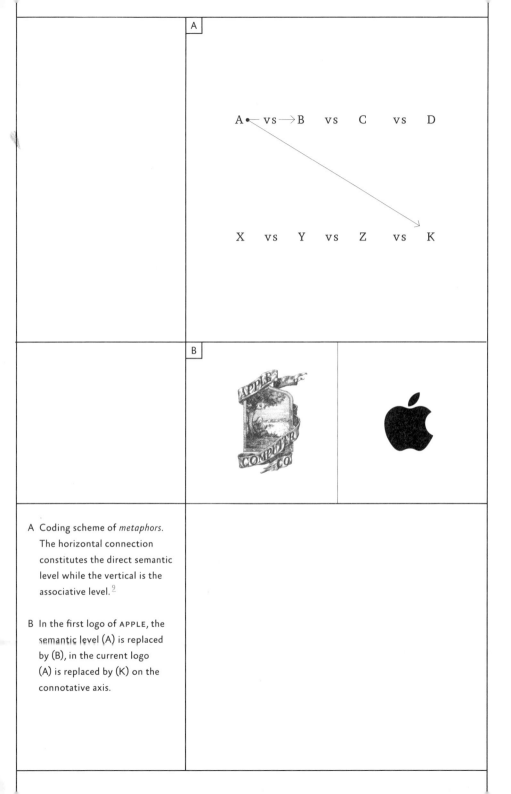

A   vs →B   vs   C   vs   D

X   vs   Y   vs   Z   vs   K

A Coding scheme of *metaphors*. The horizontal connection constitutes the direct semantic level while the vertical is the associative level. [9]

B In the first logo of APPLE, the semantic level (A) is replaced by (B), in the current logo (A) is replaced by (K) on the connotative axis.

B — IV   A $\longleftrightarrow$ B

Metonymy

The Greek word *metōnymía* literally translates into "change of name". In the "Rhetorica ad Herennium" (Rhetoric: For Herennius), *metonymy* is called "denominatio", Latin for denomination. "Metonymy uses related or contiguous concepts to establish an understanding of a subject that is not mentioned by its own name." [10] The words "related" and "contiguous" reveal the difference to *metaphors*. The associative relationship is not created by a third comparison but through a real relationship with the actual term. [11] The relationship between the words consists of a *causal, spatial,* or *temporal* interrelation. [12] *Metonymy* therefore consists of two parts: the actual term (A) and the related term that is used instead (B).

In a *causal relationship,* the cause may be stated while the effect is meant or vice versa. There are two ways for relating terms to each other: using the inventor to represent the invention or the raw material to represent the product, or vice versa. An example of the first case is "Driving a <u>Ford</u>." In this case the inventor, Henry Ford, represents the invention, the car. An example of the raw material representing the product is used by Friedrich Schiller: "Go—you have become the greatest Roman, since your <u>iron</u> plunged in your father's breast [...]". In this case, iron (the raw product) represents the dagger (product). [13]

B—IV   A *spatial relationship* also offers two options for substitution. Either the vessel represents the contents or the location stands
for its residents. [14] For example: "With this, he handed Socrates the
cup" (Plato) instead of "With this, he handed Socrates the poison."
The vessel (cup) represents the contents (poison). [15] Similarly, in the
statement "Rio de Janeiro is in a state of emergency", the location
(Rio de Janeiro) represents its residents. [16]

             In a *temporal relationship*, the time period represents the
people in the respective era. "The 16th century experienced a revival."
Beyond any doubt, in this case the people living at that time are meant. [17]

Abstraction

The logo of a company contains in its figurative and/or word mark an object that has
a *causal, spatial* or *temporal relationship* to
the company. *Metonymy* is used to transcribe
specific characteristics of a company which, as opposed to *metaphors*,
have a factual basis. When abstracted into a logo, the company can be
represented by both the inventor or the invention *(causal)*, as well as
the vessel or its contents *(spatial)*. One example of a company name
being derived from an invention is XEROX. The name is directly
derived from xerography, a printing method. In BOSCH, on the other
hand, the name of the inventor represents the company. It is also
possible for a logo to contain both the vessel and the content. An
example of this is JACOBS. The J of the word mark is shaped like a
coffee cup, while the curved line indicates the contents.

             In a *causal relationship*, therefore, the company can be
symbolized by the inventor (BOSCH) or the invention (XEROX), the
raw material (ERCO) or the product (FSB).

A   In the XEROX logo the inven-
    tion represents the company
    (causal relationship).

B   The founder Robert Bosch rep-
    resents the company BOSCH.
    Another example of *metonymy*
    (causal relationship).

C   The JACOBS logo contains a
    *metonymy (spatial relation-
    ship)*. Both the vessel and the
    content are visualized.

D   Light, not luminaries.
    The ERCO logo is an example
    in which the raw material
    represents the company.

E   FSB, a manufacturer of door
    handles, is an example of a
    product representing the
    company—*metonymy (causal
    relationship)*.

A	B
xerox	BOSCH

C	D
JACOBS	ERCO

E	
FSB	

B — IV

In a *spatial relationship*, the vessel and content can be additionally subdivided. For the vessel, there are the following options: earth (AT&T), state (TEXAS INSTRUMENTS), region (AMAZON),[18] city (PORSCHE), house (CASA DA MÚSICA), body (INTUIT), body part (TIME WARNER), or object (TCHIBO). The content can be, for example, subdivided into various counterparts of the vessel. For example, for earth (vessel) the matching content can be water, human being, or animal.

Depending on the task at hand, the subdivisions can be expanded further or replaced by other terms. There are no creative limits to this process. For example, when designing a logo for an opera house, the building as well as the meaning could be treated as a vessel and the voice treated as the content.

In a *temporal relationship* it is possible to visualize objects that are characteristic of a certain era in the logo. For example, the logo of DEUTSCHE POST contains a horn as a signal instrument, which recalls the early days of postal delivery. It is also possible to use persons of a specific century in the logo, as practiced by the QUAKER OATS COMPANY.

A The logo of AT&T features the globe, a *metonymy (causal relationship)*, while TEXAS INSTRUMENTS refers to its place of origin in its figurative mark, which is also a *metonymy (spatial relationship)*.	**A**
B The online retailer AMAZON refers to the variety (of species) in the rain forest. The PORSCHE logo refers to the city emblem of Stuttgart. In both logos a *metonymy (spatial relationship)* is used.	**B**
C The concert hall CASA DA MÚSICA is an example of a *metonymy (spatial relationship)*, related to the building (vessel). The software manufacturer INTUIT uses the body as a vessel.	**C**
D A *metonymy (spatial relationship)* is also used in the figurative mark of TIME WARNER CABLE (eye and ear) and TCHIBO (coffee bean).	**D**
E Examples of *metonymy (temporal relationship)*: The logo of the QUAKER OATS COMPANY and DEUTSCHE POST.	**E**

B — IV   a   ⟷   A

Synecdoche

The word *synekdoché* is of Greek origin and literally translated means "simultaneous understanding". In rhetoric, *synecdoche* is a special form of *metonymy*. However, in contrast to *metonymy*, the relationship between the two terms is not *causal, spatial,* or *temporal,* but only representative. A part represents the whole, or vice versa. [19]

> "The Eyes around—had wrung them dry—
> And Breaths were gathering firm
> For that last Onset—when the King
> Be witnessed—in the Room" (E. Dickinson)

In this example, a part (the eyes) is stated, but the whole (person) is meant. In comparison, in the following example, the whole represents the part: "The church, the state, the school, the magazine, think they are liberal and free! It is the freedom of a prison-yard!" (H. D. Thoreau). The church, state, school and magazine represent the people who administer them and who belong to them. Therefore, the *synecdoche* consists of two elements, the part (a) and the whole (A).

B — IV

Abstraction

The picture or word mark of a logo contains an object that features part of a product or a service, which represents the whole, or vice versa. As mentioned above, *synecdoche* is a special form of *metonymy*, which makes it difficult to draw a clear distinguishing line between these two. One possibility for differentiation is to use the *synecdoche* to explicitly refer to a product or service. In this case, showing a part or a whole in the word and figurative marks to highlight specific characteristics of products or services.

An example in which a part represents the whole is the logo of FINISH, a company specialized in individual packaging. The colon that is created of the two missing i-dots indicates a to do list. The list (part) represents the whole, i.e. the organized completion of individual tools. [20] The opposite is applied by the construction company HOCHTIEF, in which the whole, structural and civil engineering indicates the activities of the company.

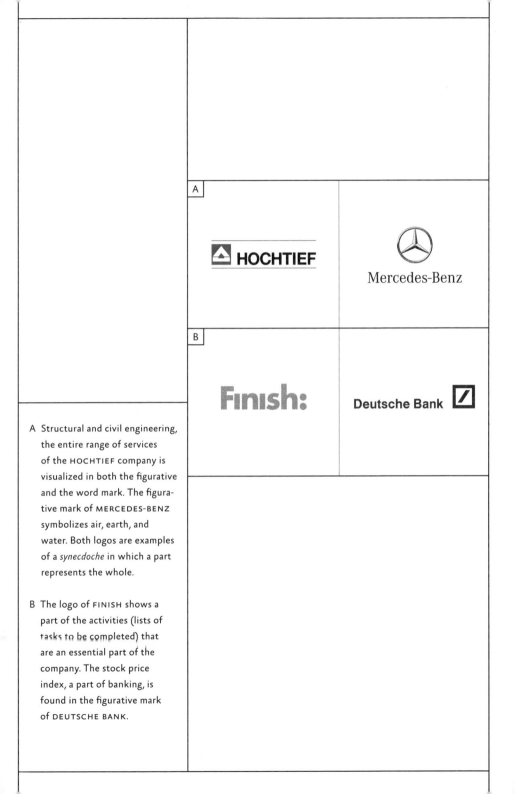

A Structural and civil engineering, the entire range of services of the HOCHTIEF company is visualized in both the figurative and the word mark. The figurative mark of MERCEDES-BENZ symbolizes air, earth, and water. Both logos are examples of a *synecdoche* in which a part represents the whole.

B The logo of FINISH shows a part of the activities (lists of tasks to be completed) that are an essential part of the company. The stock price index, a part of banking, is found in the figurative mark of DEUTSCHE BANK.

B—IV   *Onomatopoeia*

[Greek *ónomă* = name + *poieīn* = bring forth, compose]

Words are phonetically presented the way they occur in nature. [21]

> "Hark! How the worm gnaws on the wood,
> hark! How the willow laments in the lake,
> buzz, buzz, buzz, regret is going round."
> (C. Bretano)

Abstraction

The logo presents the sounds in the way they appear in nature.

EN
O

knaben
chor
gütersloh

A The ENGLISH NATIONAL OPERA
and the GÜTERSLOH BOYS' CHOIR
each employ sound mimicry.

B—IV   *Emphasis*

_____

[Greek *émphăsis* = visualization; stress]

Emphasis is the special accentuation of a word or sentence. In writing, *emphasis* is marked by exclamation marks, italics or underlining. [22]

> "Max and Moritz ! I grow sick, When I think on your last trick !" (W. Busch)

_____

Abstraction

In logos, letters or words are emphasized in arbitrary locations.

A

northernireland
tourist board

WOHNFLEX

ESADE

FONDS
PODIUM
KUNSTEN
PERFORMING
ARTS FUND **NL**

A Highlighting by *emphasis*. In the
   NORTHERN IRELAND TOURIST
   BOARD logo the *emphasis* is
   in the choice of color. The
   ESADE UNIVERSITY uses a
   different font and size. The
   same is applied by WOHNFLEX
   and the art foundation FONDS
   PODIUMKUNSTEN.

B — IV   *Euphemism*

[Greek *eúphämos* = the use of words of good omen]

An *euphemism* is an innocuous word that is used instead of words
that are considered offensive or unpleasant. [23]

> "Of this, he had to <u>die</u>—I mean <u>pass away</u>."
> (Jean Paul)

Abstraction

In logos, especially in the figurative mark,
elements and objects are used that embellish
facts or vividly illustrate them.

WWF

bp

A The logo of WWF generates empathy and thus catches attention.

B In contrast, the BP logo deliberately uses positive associations (Helios symbol) to cast itself in a better light

B—IV   *Hyperbole*

[Greek *hyperbolä* = exaggeration]

Hyperbole is the deliberate exaggeration of facts. This can be achieved by magnification or diminution. [24]

> "I am <u>bursting</u> with joy today."
> "At a <u>snail's pace</u>."
> "A mouth like a <u>barn door</u>."
> (C. Ottmers)

Abstraction   In logos, certain letters, words or shapes are disproportionately accentuated.

A

moⷦr

PIRELLI

HE**MU**

m_{ini}**useum**_{ürren}

A Creating attention by
exaggeration. This is possible
by using the *hyperbole*. The
logos of MOOR (construction),
PIRELLI (tire manufacturer),
the Swiss musical academy
HEMU and MINI MUSEUM
MÜRREN employ this device.

B—IV   *Alliteration*

———————————

[Latin *ăd* = at, near + *lītteră* = letter of the alphabet]

Alliteration is the repetition of the first consonant sound within a sentence. Either all letters are the same within a sentence, or the consonants are repeated irregularly within a sentence. [25]

> "The fair breeze blew, the white foam flew,
> The furrow followed free;
> We were the first that ever burst
> Into that silent sea." (S. T. Coleridge)

———————————

Abstraction

With *alliteration*, the logo of a company contains the same consonant at the beginning of each word within the word mark, or the first consonant of the word mark is repeated in the figurative mark.

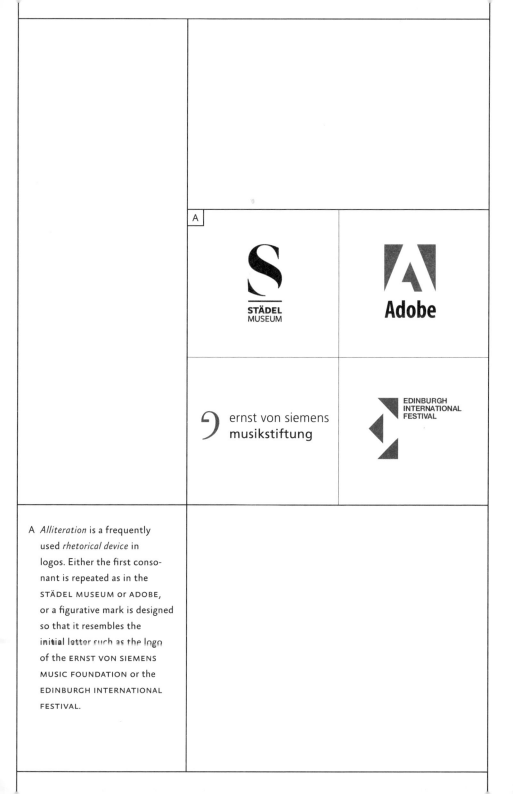

A

STÄDEL MUSEUM

Adobe

ernst von siemens
musikstiftung

EDINBURGH
INTERNATIONAL
FESTIVAL

A *Alliteration* is a frequently
used *rhetorical device* in
logos. Either the first consonant is repeated as in the
STÄDEL MUSEUM or ADOBE,
or a figurative mark is designed
so that it resembles the
initial letter such as the logo
of the ERNST VON SIEMENS
MUSIC FOUNDATION or the
EDINBURGH INTERNATIONAL
FESTIVAL.

B — IV   *Anaphora*

_____

[Greek *anăphŏrā* = carrying back]

An *anaphora* is the repetition of part of a word, a word, or a group of words at the beginning of sentences or units of speech. [26]

> "It was the best of times, it was the worst
> of times, it was the age of wisdom, it was
> the age of foolishness, it was the epoch of
> belief, it was the epoch of incredulity, it
> was the season of Light, it was the season of
> Darkness, it was the spring of hope, it was
> the winter of despair." (C. Dickens)

> "Five years have passed;
> Five summers, with the length of
> Five long winters! and again I hear
> these waters ..." (W. Wordsworth)

_____

Abstraction

In logos, the first letters of the word mark or the same word is repeated in the figurative mark or word mark.

WÜRTH

BLAUPUNKT

APDI

TILT

A In the logo of WÜRTH, the first two letters are repeated in the figurative mark, and the entire word mark in the logos of BLAUPUNKT, APDI and TILT.

B — IV   *Polyptoton*

[Greek *polýs* = many, numerous + *ptōsĭs* = case]

A *polyptoton* is the repetition of the words of the same root within a closed context with a different inflection or conjugation. [27]

> "With eager <u>feeding</u> <u>food</u> doth choke the feeder." (W. Shakespeare)

> "<u>Absolute</u> power corrupts <u>absolutely</u>." (Lord Acton)

Abstraction

In logos, elements are repeated in a different form.

corilon

AAYA

boskke

BREE

A In the *polyptoton scheme*,
shapes are repeated in an
altered form, such as the logos
of CORILON (workshop for
violin construction/restoration),
AAYA (restaurant chain),
BOSKKE (indoor gardening) and
BREE (bags and accessories).

B — IV   *Diaphora*

———————————

[Greek *diăphorā* = difference, to tear apart]

Diaphora is the random repetition of letters of a word or group of words at another location. [28]

> "That lie shall lie so heavy on my sword,
> That it shall render vengeance and revenge
> Till thou the lie-giver and that lie do lie
> In earth as quiet as thy father's skull."
> (W. Shakespeare)

> "The king is dead. Long live the king."

———————————

Abstraction

In logos, letters or parts of words are highlighted and repeated elsewhere in word marks or figurative marks.

ARTERIA

↑ntegr↓ty

RA/NY
C/TY
STOR/ES

THE C◯MPANY
B◯◯KS

A Similar to *alliteration, diaphora*
is the repetition of letters.
In the logos of ARTERIA and
INTEGRITY these are the
vastly altered letters a and i.
In RAINY CITY STORIES and
THE COMPANY BOOKS there are
slightly altered letters i and o.

B—IV   ## Climax and anticlimax

[Greek *klīmax* = staircase or ladder, graduated ascend]

Climax or *anticlimax* is a gradual ascent or descent in presenting a statement. [29]

> "Beauty is but a vain and doubtful good;
> A shining gloss that vadeth suddenly;
> A flower that dies when first it gins to bud;
> A brittle glass that's broken presently:
> A doubtful good, a gloss, a glass, a flower,
> <u>Lost, vaded, broken, dead within an hour.</u>"
> (W. Shakespeare)

> "This note was a promise that all <u>men</u>, yes, <u>black men</u> as well as <u>white men</u>, would be guaranteed the unalienable Rights of Life, Liberty and the pursuit of Happiness."
> (M. L. King)

Abstraction   In logos, individual elements are gradually increased or decreased.

A The *schemes climax* and *anticlimax* are frequently used *rhetorical devices*. It can be seen in the logos of LIIF, ERCO, ENO and BEST.

92   A LANGUAGE FOR THE SHAPE
SCHEMES—TRANSPOSITION
     RHETORIC OF LOGOS

B—IV   *Parenthesis*

[Greek *părenthesis* = to place alongside, to insert]

A *parenthesis* is a sentence that is placed outside the basic sentence structure but is part of the thought. [30]

> "Even losing you (<u>the</u> joking <u>voice, a</u> gesture
> <u>I love</u>) I shan't have lied. It's evident
> the art of losing's not too hard to master
> though it may look like (<u>Write it!</u>) like
> disaster." (E. Bishop)

Abstraction   Additional letters, shapes or colours are integrated into the word mark of a logo.

Mobil

BRAUN

FREED

PELIƒILIP

w€ekend

m

A In the *transposition scheme parenthesis* typographical elements and shapes are enlarged or inserted. For example in the logos of MOBIL, BRAUN, PETER FREED, PELIFILIP, WEEKEND and MOTHERCARE.

B — IV   *Anastrophe*

———————

[Greek *ănăstrophä* = turning back or about]

Anastrophe is the inversion of the syntax of words and entire
sentences by rearranging the normal order. [31]

> "He holds him with his skinny hand,
> 'There was a ship,' quoth he.
> 'Hold off! unhand me, grey-beard loon!'
> Eftsoons his hand dropt he."
> (S. T. Coleridge)

> "Joined the Dark Side, Dooku has.
> Lies, deceit, creating mistrust are his
> ways now." (Yoda)

———————— In logos, letters are twisted or mirrored.

Abstraction

MORE TH>N

act:onaid

A Changing the position of
letters alters the meaning.
In the MORE THAN logo this
is achieved by a 45 degree
rotation, in the ACTIONAID
logo by a 90 degree rotation.

B — IV   *Ellipsis*

[Greek *élleipsis* = omission]

Ellipsis refers to the omission of words or sentence parts. [32]

> "The vast flapping sheet flattened itself out,
> and each shove of the brush revealed fresh
> legs, hoops, horses, glistening reds and blues,
> beautifully smooth, until half the wall was
> covered with the advertisement of a circus;
> a hundred horsemen, twenty performing
> seals, lions, tigers ... Craning forwards, for
> she was short-sighted, she read it out ... 'will
> visit this town,' she read." (V. Woolf)

Abstraction

In logos, letters or parts of letters are omitted.

A

A Omissions create attention, for example in the logos of OYUNA and MULTICANAL. The logos gain additional context as seen in the logo of MAMA SHELTER and FEDEX.

[1] The classification of the *rhetorical devices* was adopted from the book "Grundriß der Rhetorik".

[2] The following *rhetorical devices* were analyzed individually for their use in design: *metaphor, metonymy, synecdoche, onomatopoeia, emphasis, euphemism, alliteration,* and *diaphora.* For *hyperbole, anaphora, polyptoton, climax,* and *anticlimax, anastrophe, parenthesis,* and *ellipsis* examples from Hanno Ehses's and Ellen Lupton's "Rhetorical Handbook" (1988) were used.

[3] Cf. Ottmers, C., 2007, 174

[4] Cf. Ottmers, C., 2007, 171

[5] Cf. Ottmers, C., 2007, 174

[6] Cf. Biedermann, H., 2004, 244

[7] Cf. Plett, H., 2001, 100f.

[8] Cf. Eco, U., 1972, 182f.

[9] Ibid.

[10] Rhetorik an Herennius, IV, 32

[11] Cf. Ueding, G., Steinbrink, B., 2011, 295

[12] Cf. Ottmers, C., 2007, 180

[13] Ibid.

[14] Ibid.

[15] Cf. Ueding, G., Steinbrink, B., 2011, 295

[16] Cf. Ottmers, C., 2007, 180

[17] Ibid.

[18] AMAZON is an exception, as due to the lack of a relationship to the Amazon it could also be classified as a *metaphor.* However, since the association to the location is easier to create, the logo is classified as a *metonymy.*

[19] Cf. Ottmers, C., 2007, 181

[20] Cf. Evamy, M., 2012, 240

[21] Cf. Harjung, D., 2000, 312

[22] Cf. Harjung, D., 2000, 161f.

[23] Cf. Harjung, D., 2000, 193f.

[24] Cf. Harjung, D., 2000, 230

[25] Cf. Harjung, D., 2000, 36

[26] Ibid.

[27] Cf. Harjung, D., 2000, 358

[28] Cf. Harjung, D., 2000, 142

[29] Cf. Harjung, D., 2000, 252

[30] Cf. Harjung, D., 2000, 336

[31] Cf. Ottmers, C., 2007, 170

[32] Cf. Harjung, D., 2000, 135

B — V   ## *Findings*

Based on the previous analysis, the following conclusions can be drawn: *tropes* and *schemes* fulfill the same functions verbally and visually. In this case, *tropes* are related to the meaning or content. They illustrate the character of a company, render messages more precise, and present statements in a novel way. They can therefore be described as content-related concepts. *Schemes*, on the other hand, are related to the form. They are form-related concepts that embellish ideas and change the normal order of elements. Almost all presented examples show that a logo can contain *tropes* as well as *schemes*. In addition, it was found that there is a causal relationship between the *rhetorical devices* (means) and the *appeal strategy* (end). Based on this, it is possible to complement the *relevance model* and deduct repeatable rules for the design process.

The presented catalog of *rhetorical devices* can be used to systematically search for solutions without having to start over for each new project. This can be applied in several ways. For example, during the initial meeting or following a briefing targeted questions can be asked about specific characteristics that are related to the company or the product. The catalog can also be used as a creative tool during brainstorming. Therefore, it is best to first resort to *tropes* to develop a basic idea. The recommended second step would then be to apply *schemes* to develop a formal idea. However, this order is not binding. The list of devices can also be used as a checklist to determine if relevant solutions have been missed.

Being familiar with the *rhetorical devices* reduces the complexity of the work process as their application creates an order. This way, a large number of logos can be categorized according to their content-related and formal aspects within a short period of time. This categorization serves as the basis for an in-depth analysis. Industry-specific approaches can be identified in a targeted manner to subsequently deliberately deviate from the industry standard, if strategically required. In addition, defining the *rhetorical devices* assists in communicating clearly. Advantages and disadvantages can be discussed more specifically as everyone involved in the discussion is referring to the same concepts. Furthermore, the vocabulary strengthens the perception of logos in everyday life that can now be reviewed with new criteria, stored in the memory, and retrieved.

At this point it must be said that, of course, these rules do not automatically lead to successful designs. The knowledge that there are seven different types of *metaphors* is no guarantee that the most suitable one will be found. The catalog presented here, however, helps to understand the design process and making it describeable to others. It offers useful information that will eliminate some of the myths, opinions and prejudices regarding communication design.

C — I   *Expansion of the relevance model*
_____

In this section the *rhetorical devices* contained in the logos will be allocated to the intended effects *presence* (P), *substance* (S) and *reference* (R) as described in the *relevance model* by Beyrow. As the intended effects overlap in some cases, the following constellations are also possible: *presence-substance, presence-reference, substance-reference,* and *presence-substance-reference.* Listing the logos in combination with the applied *rhetorical devices* will indicate which *device* is responsible for which target effect.

According to Beyrow, the criteria with which this can be accomplished can be described as follows:

› Logos that create a *presence* are distinguished by form, color, dimension, and weight. However, they do not visualize aspects related to the contents of the company.[1]
› Logos that create *substance* convey the core business area of the company. They provide information regarding the output of the company.[2]
› Logos that generate *reference* create links to established values from other areas that nevertheless have no factual relevance to the company.[3]

Presence	● **BLAUPUNKT** Consumer electronics Synecdoche [P], anaphora [P]

 Adobe Software company Alliteration [P]	 **STÄDEL** MUSEUM Art museum Alliteration [P]	oʝuna Fashion company Ellipsis [P]
ΛΛΥΛ Restaurant chain Polyptoton [P]	TILT Video and graphic design Anaphora [P]	APDƗ Professional association Anaphora [P]
 RAINY CITY STORIES Online collection of literature Metonymy [P], diaphora [P]	**ARTERIΛ** Artist network Diaphora [P]	PELI*f*ILIP Law office Parenthesis [P]
Mobil Oil company Parenthesis [P]	BRAUN Electronics manufacturer Metonymy [S], parenthesis [P]	┃IRELLI Tire manufacturer Hyperbole [P]

ESADE University Emphasis [P]	**Presence-Substance**	
GREENPEACE Environmental protection agency Metaphor [P] [S]	at&t Telecommunications Metonymy [P] [S]	ernst von siemens **musikstiftung** Music foundation Metonymy [S], alliteration [P] [S]
EDINBURGH INTERNATIONAL FESTIVAL Art festival Metonymy [S], alliteration [P] [S]	northernireland tourist board Tourist board Metonymy [S], emphasis [P] [S]	**FONDS** **PODIUM** **KUNSTEN** PERFORMING ARTS FUND **NL** Art foundation Metonymy [S], emphasis [P]
mo⌒r House constructor Metonymy [S], hyperbole [P] [S]	**m**ini**USEUM**dürren Museum Metonymy [S], hyperbole [P] [S]	**ER**CO Lamp manufacturer Metonymy [S], anticlimax [P] [S]
  Social investment fund Metonymy [S], climax [P] [S]	 Boys' choir Metonymy [S], climax [P] [S], onomatopoeia [P] [S]	EN O State opera Metonymy [S], climax [P] [S], onomatopoeia [P] [S]

Retailer Metonymy [S], parenthesis [P] [S]	Indoor gardening Metonymy [S], polyptoton [P] [S]	Retailer Metonymy [P] [S], synecdoche [P] [S]

Telecommunications Metonymy [P] [S], synecdoche [S]	Logistics Synecdoche [S], ellipsis [P] [S]	Concert hall Metonymy [P] [S]
 WWF	FREED	BREE
Environmental protection agency Synecdoche [S], euphemism [P] [S]	Photographer Synecdoche [S], parenthesis [P] [S]	Bags and accessories Synecdoche [S], polyptoton [P] [S]
coslon	intuit.	act:onaid
Violin specialist store Synecdoche [S], polyptoton [P] [S]	Software manufacturer Metonymy [S], ellipsis [P]	Environmental protection agency Anastrophe [P] [S]
MORE TH>N	BEST	THE C MPANY BOOKS
Insurance Anastrophe [P] [S]	Supermarket Climax [P] [S]	Bookkeeping and business accounting Diaphora [P] [S]

↑ntegr↓ty Management consulting Diaphora [P] [S]	**WOHN**FLEX Furniture store Emphasis [P] [S]	HE**MU** Musical academy Hyperbole [P] [S]
  TV channel Parenthesis [P] [S]	*Presence-Reference*	
 Multicanal Cable network operator Metaphor [R], alliteration [P], ellipsis [P]	 Power company Metaphor [R] [P], euphemism [P]	 Automobile manufacturer Metaphor [R] [P]
  Automobile manufacturer Metaphor [R]	 Automobile manufacturer Metaphor [R] [P]	 Sports equipment manufacturer Metaphor [R] [P]
  Product design company Metaphor [R] [P]	 Fashion company Metaphor [R] [P]	 Computer manufacturer Metaphor [R] [P]

 penguin Publishing house Metaphor [R] [P]	 Automobile manufacturer Metonymy [R] [P]	 Food manufacturer Metonymy [R] [P]
Presence-Substance-Reference		 Design hotel Metaphor [P] [R] [S], ellipsis [P] [R] [S]
Substance-Reference		 Mercedes-Benz Automobile manufacturer Metaphor [R], metonymy [S], synecdoche [S]
amazon Online retailer Metonymy [S] [R]	*Substance*	
FSB Door handle manufacturer Metonymy [S]	JACOBS Coffee manufacturer Metonymy [S]	Deutsche Post Logistics Metonymy [S]

Industrial company
Metonymy [S], synecdoche [S]

Business services
Metonymy [S], alliteration [S]

Construction company
Synecdoche [S]

Deutsche Bank

Bank
Synecdoche [S]

Packaging manufacturer
Synecdoche [S], ellipsis [S]

Reference

Bank
Metaphor [R]

citi

Bank
Metaphor [R]

LINCOLN

Automobile manufacturer
Metaphor [R]

Electronics store chain
Metaphor [R]

Electronics manufacturer
Metonymy [R]

WÜRTH

Assembly technology
Metonymy [R], anaphora [R]

[1] Cf. Beyrow, M., 2013, 268f.

[2] Ibid.

[3] Ibid.

C — II   *Locations and instructions*

TROPES

Metaphor

Find a similarity between the company and another area that is not factually related to it. Base your decision on the following categories: nature metaphors, color metaphors, mineralogical metaphors, cosmological metaphors, body part metaphors, nautical metaphors, mythological metaphors and object metaphors.

Onomatopoeia

Find sounds that occur in nature and represent them in the design.

Synecdoche

Focus on the products or services of the company. Find a part that describes the whole or vice versa.

_____

Emphasis

*Emphasize individual
letters in the word mark.*

*Emphasize a word in the
word mark.*

*Emphasize individual
elements of the
figurative mark.*

_____

Hyperbole

*Emphasize letters, words
or shapes by presenting
them disproportionately
large or small.*

_____

Euphemism

*Find trivializing words
and implement them in
the figurative mark.*

_____

Metonymy

*Find a relation to the
company that has a factual
basis. This basis can be
causal, spatial or temporal.
With a spatial relation-
ship you can make a list
that includes all vessels.
This may include all objects
that concern the company
and its products or services.
Allocate the suitable
content to each vessel.*

C — II

Anaphora

*Visualize the first letters
of the word mark in the
figurative mark.*

*Emphasize the first
letters or the word mark
by formal means.*

Polyptoton

*Repeat similar elements in
an altered form.*

*Repeat elements of a letter
in an altered form.*

*Look for a relationship
between a letter and an
object and repeat the
object in an altered form.*

SCHEMES—ADDITION

Alliteration

*Repeat the first letter.
Emphasize it by formal
means.*

*Create a figurative mark
from the first letter and
an object.*

Climax and anticlimax

*Strengthen or weaken
letters gradually by
changing the font or
sizes and gradation
of colors.*

*Treat the forms in the
same way by modifying
the size or color gradation.*

Ellipsis

Position individual letters
negatively.

Replace a punch by a form
or an object. Use forms
to create a negative letter.

Take a close look at
the spaces of the word
and integrate a form
or an object.

Parenthesis

Insert additional forms or
letters among the individual letters.

Integrate additional forms
or individual letters in a
character.

Emphasize an individual
letter within a word group
by using a different font.

Emphasize an individual
letter within a word group
by enlarging it or using
italics or gradation.

Diaphora

Repeat letters or word
segments in another place.

Emphasize letters or word
segments in another place.

Anastrophe

Twist or mirror individual
letters.

Causing an effect—
The ultimate aim of a successful logo

It is not always easy to defend a logo design. There are several reasons for this, one major reason is the fact that there are insufficient criteria for evaluation. Insufficient because the terms simplicity, succinctness and memorability can be perceived and interpreted in different ways and are therefore ill-suited for argumentation. Thus, what is missing is a method of analysis that is based on formal-esthetic and communicative effect principles. These are the key aspects of a logo. From its outset, rhetoric has been focusing on the principles of effect. Accordingly, we not only looked at the effect of words but also of images and signs. The strategies discovered in this process are summarized under *Modes of persuasion of a speech*. In the following sections we introduce a method of analysis[1] for the evaluation of logos based on the terms and methods of rhetoric.

The four viewpoints — In summary, a complete analysis or description of the effect of a logo consists of four steps. First, the arrangement of the elements is inspected *(1)* and only then the effects of the *stylistic devices* are examined *(2)*. The next step focuses on the effects of the *rhetorical devices* *(3)*. In conclusion it is determined on c — iii   which mode of persuasion level *(logos, ethos, pathos)* the logo communicates *(4)*. The process described briefly here will be explained in greater detail in the following section.

(1) **_Visual stimulation_**   As described in the previous section, at first glance, the attention is drawn exclusively to the arrangement of the *stylistic devices* and not on the intended meaning level. This type of observation is independent of culture and has the same effect on every individual.[2] However, since most logos are composed according to the same principle—locomotive principle (the figurative mark is placed left of the word mark), push principle (the word mark is placed left of the figurative mark), the star principle (the figurative mark shines like a star above the word mark), the anchor principle (the figurative mark is below the word mark), the rail car principle (the figurative mark is positioned in the middle of the word mark), and the island principle (the figurative mark and the word mark are clearly separated from each other)[3] —the observation is not always very fruitful.

⟨ Six principles to compose a logo. From left to right, top to bottom: locomotive principle, push principle, star principle, anchor principle, rail car principle and island principle

Example: The logo of GÜTERSLOH BOYS' CHOIR is excellently suited to describe these effects. The arrangement of the lowercase letters is dynamic, chaotic and hectic. The two Os are visually prominent due to their color and size and catch one's attention.

(2) <u>*Concrete effects*</u>   In a second step the effects of the *stylistic devices* are described. The observation, and thus the effect of the logo, depends on cultural influences, personal experiences and individual characteristics.[4]

Example: The bold Futura used in the logo of industrial machine manufacturer VOITH appears robust, strong, massive and masculine. The clear shapes of the font appear objective, neutral, simple, and modern. The color blue used by VOITH symbolizes trust.

C — III

(3) Expression and attitude This is followed by an examination of the effects that are caused by the originator, i.e. the company. In this type of analysis the effect is mainly caused by the *rhetorical devices* and less so by the graphic elements. [5] The question that should be posed here is: What is the message that the company intends to send via the logo? For example, the APPLE logo does not provide direct information about the company's services and is thus enigmatic, which in turn fosters curiosity and interest in the company. The recipient is asked to decipher the logo. As various associations are possible, the company appears mysterious. The idea of using such a figurative mark for identification is undoubtedly inventive. This makes the company appear smart and creative.

(4) Modes of persuasion and rhetorical appeal In the fourth and final step the results of the previous sections are summarized and allocated to one, sometimes also several, *modes of persuasion.* Rhetoric distinguishes three, occasionally overlapping, modes *(logos, ethos, pathos).*

Using the objective factual mode *(logos),* the logo appeals to the observer by showing the association with the industry sector or presentation of the produced product. As soon as the values of a company are at the core of the communication, there is a transition to the *ethos* mode. For example, the theme could be the company's dedication to environmental protection. In the *pathos* mode, the aim is to evoke specific emotions. There is a wide range of emotions. When it comes to logos, the relevant emotions are: interest, curiosity, surprise, exhilaration, friendliness, sympathy, self-confidence, hope, trust, security, goodwill, and pride. By not being clearly allocated to its sector, the APPLE logo can evoke curiosity and interest in the company. It can also convey a feeling of hope and trust, such as the word mark of LIIF, a fund for socially disadvantaged individuals.

We should also mention the opposite, negatively charged emotions, which are usually unintentionally evoked by logos: boredom, indifference, rejection, anger, disappointment, disgust, overload, confusion, paternalism, mistrust and shame.

It is not always easy to differentiate between *ethos* and *pathos appeals* as they partially overlap. The "Historisches Wörterbuch der Rhetorik" (Historical dictionary of rhetoric) contains a helpful definition. It defines the *ethos appeal* as causing a mild emotion over an extended period of time, while the effect of the *pathos appeal* is immediate and brief.[6]

Analysis

_____

To illustrate the analysis method, three logos are discussed in detail below. The focus of the analysis is to determine the methods of persuasion to draw conclusions about the way the logos appeal to the observer and how they achieve their intended effects. As we shall see later, while logos convey specific effects, they have only limited capacities for creating an effective interplay of effects. This only emerges in combination with the other components of the corporate design and the corporation itself. For this reason it is all the more important to consciously synchronize and combine the different effects.

_____

Method

In the first step, the logos were examined based on the four described steps and the effects noted manually. In the next step, lacking terminology was complemented with the help of a list of various effects.[7] After a certain amount of time, the notes were compared to the logo and revised where required. During the entire process, great care was taken to remain objective. Nevertheless, the results are subjective impressions that must be verified or falsified in a next step by test subjects to test the derived theses.

C — IV   *FSB*
_____

⌐ FSB

(1) Visual stimulation

organized, clearly structured, uniform

(2) Concrete effect

Color: objective, neutral

Font: objective, neutral, unpretentious, simple

Shape: objective, neutral, simple

(3) Expression and attitude

rational, informative, logical, modest,

authentic, credible

(4) Mode of persuasion

logos: factual, informative

FSB is a manufacturer of door and window handles. The abbreviation is a combination of the name of the founder (Franz Schneider) and the company's place of business (Brakel).

(1) On the visual stimulation level the logo appears organized. The handle is slightly visually prominent due to the use of a thicker line width.

(2) The color of the logo, the font and the shape appear objective, neutral, unpretentious, and simple.

(3) The logo contains three incidences of *metonymy*, which have a purely factual character in this context. The conveyed message is "Franz Schneider of Brakel manufactures door handles." The effects that can be associated with the originator can be described as rational, informative, logical, modest, authentic, and credible.

(4) The logo therefore addresses the *logos* mode exclusively and is a suitable example to demonstrate that it is not entirely devoid of emotions. The objectivity and target orientation expressed in the logo reflects the attitude of the company and aims to establish trust in the long run. However, at the same time there is the danger of the logo not being recognized due to its sober nature.

C — IV   *MAMA SHELTER*

(1) *Visual stimulation*
Focused on the word mark and the white space
between the chicken legs.

(2) *Concrete effect*

Color: neutral, understated

Font: objective, modern

Shape: unusual, noticeable, amusing, humorous, creative

(3) *Expression and attitude*
attention catching, appealing, challenging, enigmatic,
plausible, amusing, humorous, creative, protected

(4) *Mode of persuasion*

ethos: humorous, creative,

pathos: curiosity, interest, amusement, protection

MAMA SHELTER is a design hotel for young people with affordable prices.

(1) By positioning the word mark between the chicken legs, the observer automatically focuses on the white space, which, upon closer inspection, turns out to be an egg.

(2) This discovery alone creates attention on the concrete effect level. In addition, the logo is distinguished by the photorealistic chicken—as opposed to iconographic representation used in other logos. The font color and font appear objective, neutral, modern and understated.

(3) While the *ellipsis* catches the attention as described above, the *metaphor* creates curiosity. The recipients are asked to search for the connection between the logo and the originator. They are given a puzzle to solve, so to speak. Resolving it creates joy and additionally the impression that it is a humorous and creative hotel, while the feeling of protective security is provided by the name of the hotel and the connection to the breeding chicken. However, this aspect does not really take effect as irony and humor prevail.

(4) The logo is primarily effective on the *pathos* level. Here, it generates interest by an *indirect metaphor*. In combination with and supported by the *ethos appeals*, this creates a humorous and extremely creative image of the hotel. The logo is unusual in every aspect and is therefore remembered.

C — IV   *LIIF*

---

(1) *Visual stimulation*
dynamic, active, vivacious

(2) *Concrete effect*
Color: vital, young, playful, refreshing, serious
Font: clear, objective
Shape: courageous, brave, self-confident

(3) *Expression and attitude*
respectful, considerate, empathic,
humane, social, motivating, integrative,
optimistic, refreshing

(4) *Mode of persuasion*
ethos: trust, confidence, goodwill
pathos: longing, hope, relief, protective security,
motivation

LIIF is the abbreviation of Low Income Investment Fund. According to its mission statement, the fund supports the poorest of the poor by investing in community-building initiatives.

(1) On the visual stimulation level, the ascending arrangement of the letters appears dynamic, active, and vivacious.

(2) This impression is continued on the concrete effect level. The colors, especially the shades of green, appear vivacious, young, playful and refreshing, while the blue appears serious. The individual letter shapes are clear and objective, their gradual ascending arrangement appears valiant, daring and self-confident.

(3) The great strengths of this logo are its semantic references that are the result of *metonymy* and the syntactic device *climax*. The smallest letter l stands for low and is detached from the other three letters. The two ascending letters i have human shapes and are intertwined, which creates the following associations in the observer: fostering each other, support each other, being there for each other, growing together, learning from each other, playing with each other. The two letters i are in turn connected to the letter f. The f stands for fund, i.e. the monetary means that the organization employs for its projects. The following message can be made regarding the three anchored letters and the detached l: "It is not important that you have limited material means. It is much more important to be there for each other. We enable this by supporting community building projects with our funds." The words respectful, considerate, self-confident, empathic, humane, social, motivating, integrating and optimistic describe the properties that are associated with the fund.

C — IV   *(4)* The logo uses several argumentation patterns at once. They present factual arguments "we support people with little income." The numerous applied *stylistic* and *rhetorical devices* merge the message with a value-based message that specifically emphasizes the character of the fund. By highlighting the character, the intention is to create trust. It emits a confident and hopeful mood coupled with goodwill. All of these emotions have a long-term lasting effect. On the direct emotional level *(pathos)* it evokes longing, hope, protective security, relief, and motivation.

[1] The analysis method is based on the work of Simon Küffer. Only individual aspects were adjusted.

[2] Cf. Küffer, S., 2014, 37

[3] Cf. Leu, O., 1992, 48f.

[4] Cf. Küffer, S., 2014, 37

[5] Ibid,

[6] Cf. Kraus, M., 2003, 690

[7] Cf. Küffer, S., 2014, 37

Findings

The analysis method led to the following findings: rhetoric's terminology is suitable for testing the potential effects of logos. They can be used to describe the level (mode) on which the *rhetorical devices* are effective. In addition, the persuasive effects resulting from the *stylistic devices* can be described in detail.

The precise difference between *ethos* and *pathos* could only be partially developed in the scope of this book. Nevertheless, additional analyses can support this differentiation. Simultaneously, an experiment should be conceived by which these assumptions can be verified. Altogether, this offers the opportunity to present the factors that affect the recipient in a detailed and differentiated way.

This method helps in applying desired effects in a targeted manner, to defend one's work, to reflect on it and to sharpen one's power of observation. However, the most important point is the chance to inform about communication design as a profession, to create transparency, and ultimately build trust.

Epilog

"Easy learning is naturally pleasant to all, and words
mean something, so that all words which make us learn
something are most pleasant." ARISTOTLE

Close inspection of the topic has uncovered the potential
of rhetoric when applied to communication design and that it is
worthwhile to examine other sciences. Becoming initially familiar
with the matter and learning the terminology is not easy at first, but
this changes once the benefits for one's own work become clear. As
confirmed by several authors and as postulated by Socrates, rhetoric
can serve as a "midwife" to design—it provides the young discipline
with the ideal theoretical base that can be applied to many problems.

At the same time, the rhetorical terms also illustrate the
importance of language. It is only possible to clearly differentiate
among objects if they are allocated to specific terms. In the professional
training of designers language usually plays a minor role. Yet, according to Wolf Lotter, it is a reliable principal witness of our intentions.
It enhances the vocabulary and helps to defend one's work, to reflect
on it and to sharpen one's powers of observation.

The knowledge gained from this book will initially play a minor role for experienced designers. For young designers, on the other hand, it offers an orientation that is helpful during training to get a grasp on complex situations and thus to understand them. The systematic approach offers them basic concepts that they can resort to and a knowledge base they can develop further—a tool kit for everyday use. However, the result is not based on the tool but on its user. What limits some, inspires others.

This primer offers an introduction to the topic, but cannot replace the individual grappling with rhetoric. It is also an appeal to designers to look beyond their own horizon and become inspired by other areas of specialization. This is not limited to rhetoric, but also includes semiotics, communication science, visual studies, and media sciences. Only with their help can communication design conceive theories of its own and mature—from an adolescent into an adult.

Bibliography

A

Aristoteles
Rhetorik
Reclam, 1999

B

Bailey, Michael D.
*A Catalogue of the Lamps
in the British Museum*
British Museum
Publications, 1980,

**Baviera, Michele /
Susin, Adrian**
*Lehrende und Lernende?
Lernende Lehren!*
Um die Ecke, 2010

**Beyrow, Matthias /
Daldrop, Norbert /
Kiedaisch, Petra**
*Corporate Identity
und Corporate Design:
das Kompendium*
AV Edition, 2013

Biedermann, Hans
Knaurs Lexikon der Symbole
AREA Verlag, 2004

**Birkigt, Klaus /
Stadler, Marinus /
Funck, Hans J.**
*Corporate Identity:
Grundlagen – Funktionen –
Fallbeispiele*
moderne industrie, 2002

Bonsiepe, Gui
*Entwurfskultur und
Gesellschaft: Gestaltung
zwischen Zentrum
und Peripherie*
Birkhäuser, 2009

Bonsiepe, Gui
»Visuell-Verbale Rhetorik
(1965, 2007)«, in: Joost, Gesche /
Scheuermann, Arne (Eds.):
*Design als Rhetorik: Grundlagen,
Positionen, Fallstudien*
Birkhäuser, 2008

Bruhn, Manfred
»Begriffliche Grundlagen
des Markenartikels und
der Markenpolitik«, in:
Bruhn, Manfred (Ed.):
*Die Marke: Symbolkraft
eines Zeichensystems*
Paul Haupt Verlag, 2001

C

Cicero, Marcus Tullius
*De oratore.
Über den Redner. Lat./Dt.*
Reclam, 1986

E

Eco, Umberto
Einführung in die Semiotik
Wilhelm Fink Verlag, 1972

Ehses, Hanno
»Rhetorik im Kommunikations-
design«, in: Joost, Gesche/
Scheuermann, Arne (Eds.):
Design als Rhetorik: Grundlagen,
Positionen, Fallstudien
Birkhäuser, 2008

Ehses, Hanno / Lupton, Ellen
Rhetorical Handbook: An Illustrated
Manual for Graphic Designers
Design Division, 1988

Evamy, Michael
TypoLogo: Mit Zeichen
Zeichen setzen!
Verlag Hermann Schmidt, 2012

F
Genzmer, Herbert
Schnellkurs Rhetorik:
Die Kunst der Rede
DuMont, 2003

G
Gerrig, Richard J. /
Zimbardo Philip G.
Psychologie
Pearson Deutschland, 2008

Göttert, Karl-Heinz
Einführung in die Rhetorik
Wilhelm Fink Verlag, 1991

H
Hamann, Sabine
Logodesign
Hüthig Jehle Rehm, 2007

Harjung, Dominik J.
Lexikon der Sprachkunst:
Die rhetorischen Stilformen.
Mit über 1000 Beispielen
C. H. Beck, 2000

J
Joost, Gesche
»Rhetorik«, in: Erlhoff, Michael/
Marshall, Timothy (Eds.),
Wörterbuch Design: Begriffliche
Perspektiven des Design
Birkhäuser Verlag, 2008

Joost, Gesche /
Scheuermann, Arne
Design als Rhetorik:
Grundlagen, Positionen,
Fallstudien
Birkhäuser, 2008

K
Kraus, Manfred
»Pathos«, in: Ueding, Gert (Ed.),
Historisches Wörterbuch der
Rhetorik, Band 6
Wissenschaftliche
Buchgesellschaft, 2003

Krippendorff, Klaus
Die semantische Wende:
Eine neue Grundlage für Design
Birkhäuser, 2012

Kroehl, Heinz
*Corporate Identity als
Erfolgsfaktor im 21. Jahrhundert*
Vahlen, 2000

Küffer, Simon
*Rhetorische Figuren im Grafikdesign:
Versuch eines systematischen und
theoretisch fundierten Katalogs*
Masterthesis Bern,
Hochschule der Künste, 2014

L
Leu, Olaf
*Corporate Design: Bestandteile
der Unternehmenskommunikation*
Novum Praxis, 1992

M
Mayr-Keber, Gert
»Strukturelemente der visuellen
Erscheinung von Corporate Identity«,
in: Birkigt, Klaus/Stadler, Marinus/
Funck, Hans J., (Eds.):
*Corporate Identity: Grundlagen –
Funktionen – Fallbeispiele*
moderne industrie, 2002

McLuhan, Marshall
*Das Medium ist die Massage:
Ein Inventar medialer Effekte
[The medium is the Massage:
An Inventory of Effects]*
Übersetzt von Baltes, Martin/
Höltschl, Rainer
Tropen, Imprint bei
Klett-Cotta, 2011

**Meffert, Heribert /
Bruhn, Manfred**
*Markenstrategien im Wettbewerb:
Eine empirische Untersuchung
zur Akzeptanz von Hersteller-,
Handels- und Gattungsmarken
(No Names)*
Gabler Verlag, 1984

Mellerowicz, Konrad
*Markenartikel: Die ökonomischen
Gesetze ihrer Preisbildung und
Preisbindung*
C.H. Beck Verlag, 1963

Mollerup, Per
*Marks of Excellence:
the history and taxonomy
of trademarks*
Phaidon Press Limited, 1997

Mollerup, Per
*Marks of Excellence:
the history and taxonomy
of trademarks*
Phaidon Press Limited, 2013

O
Ong, Walter J.
*Oralität und Literalität: die
Technologisierung des Wortes*
Westdeutscher Verlag, 1987

P
Plett, Heinrich F.
*Einführung in die
rhetorische Textanalyse*
Helmut Buske Verlag, 2001

Q

Quietude, Fitzgerald K.
in: *Erstes Design
Forschungssymposium,
14., 15. Mai 2004*
Swiss Design Network (SDN), 2005

S

Schneider, Beat
*Design – eine Einführung:
Entwurf im sozialen,
kulturellen und
wirtschaftlichen Kontext*
Birkhäuser Verlag, 2005

Shaughnessy, Adrian
*FHK Henrion:
The Complete Designer*
Unit Editions, 2013

Stankowski, Anton
»Das Visuelle Erscheinungsbild
der Corporate Identity«, in:
Birkigt, Klaus / Stadler, Marinus /
Funck, Hans J. (Eds.):
*Corporate Identity: Grundlagen –
Funktionen – Fallbeispiele*
moderne industrie, 2002

Steinbrink, Bernd / Ueding, Gert
*Grundriß der Rhetorik:
Geschichte – Technik – Methode*
Metzler, 2011

W

Wiedemann, Julius
Logo Design 2
Taschen, 2009

Without author
*Brockhaus. Enzyklopädie.
24 Bände.* (20th edition,
published 1996–1999,
taking into account the
German spelling reform).
Brockhaus, 1996

Wolfenstine, Manfred R.
Brands and Marks
University of
Oklahoma Press, 1970

Internet sources

Friedrich, Volker
*Sprache für die Form:
Forum für Design und Rhetorik*
www.designrhetorik.de
Constance, 2012

Credits

The logos in this book are used as examples of logos in general. All logos and other intellectual property referenced in this book are the property of their respective owners. Despite diligent efforts, the designer or design agency of some logos could not be identified (denoted by "designer unknown"). I apologize in advance for any errors that may have occurred in the bibliography.

A

AAYA, NORTH, 2010, pp. 87, 105
ABB, PENTAGRAM, Fletcher, Alan, 1987, p. 21
ACTIONAID, CDT DESIGN, 2006, pp. 95, 107
ADOBE, in-house design team, 1993, pp. 83, 105
AEG, Behrens, Peter, 1908, p. 19
AMAZON, TURNER DUCKWORTH, 2000, pp. 35, 69, 109
APDI, Eskenazi, Mario, 2010, pp. 85, 105
APPLE, REGIS MCKENNA ADVERTISING, Janoff, Rob, 1977; modified 1998, in-house design team, pp. 35, 63, 108, 120
APPLE, Wayne, Ronald, 1976, p. 63
ARTERIA, NORTH, 2009, pp. 89, 105
AT&T, Bass, Saul, 1983; modified 2005, INTERBRAND, pp. 69, 106
AUDI, META DESIGN, van der Laan, Paul/ van Rosmalen, Pieter, 2009, p. 31

B

BAYER, Schneider, Hans, 1900, p. 19
BEST, CHERMAYEFF & GEISMAR, 1979, pp. 49, 91, 107
BLAUPUNKT, designer unknown, pp. 85, 105
BOSCH, UNITED DESIGNERS, 2004, pp. 67, 110
BOSKKE, BIBLIOTHÈQUE, 2010, pp. 87, 107
BP, LANDOR, 2000, pp. 79, 108
BRAUN, Schmittel, Wolfgang, 1952, pp. 93, 105

BREE, BÜRO UEBELE, Schönhaar, Sabine/ Uebele, Andreas, 2008, pp. 87, 107

C

C&A, FACTOR DESIGN, SAFFRON, 2011, p. 49
CASA DA MÚSICA, SAGMEISTER INC., Sagmeister, Stefan/Ernstberger, Matthias/ Ammer, Ralph/Walesch, Quentin, 2007, pp. 69, 107
Chrkl, p. 18 (Guilds' coats of arms), CC BY 3.0
CITI BANK, PENTAGRAM, Scher, Paula, 1999, pp. 61, 110
COCA-COLA, property of COCA-COLA, p. 30
COCA-COLA, Robinson, Frank M., 1887; modified 1968, LIPPINCOTT MERCER, p. 35
CORILON, LOCKSTOFF DESIGN, Coenen, Susanne/Slink, Nicole, 2010, pp. 87, 107

D

DACIA, designer unknown, 2008, p. 20
DEUTSCHE BANK, Stankowski, Anton, 1974, pp. 20, 73, 110
DEUTSCHE POST, NITSCH DESIGN, 1998, pp. 69, 109
DR. OETKER, Kind, Theodor, 1899, p. 19
DÜSSELDORF, BBDO, 2012, p. 21

E

Eco, Umberto, p. 62 (Coding scheme)
EDINBURGH INTERNATIONAL FESTIVAL, HAT-TRICK, Howat, Gareth/Sutherland, Jim/ Swatridge, Alex, 2009, pp. 83, 106
ENGLISH NATIONAL OPERA, CDT DESIGN, Dempsey, Mike, 1991, pp. 75, 91, 106
ERCO, Aicher, Otl, 1974, pp. 67, 91, 106
ERNST VON SIEMENS MUSIC FOUNDATION, JÄGER UND JÄGER, 2009, pp. 83, 106
ESADE UNIVERSITY, SUMMA, Marnich, Wladimir/Cortada, Eduardo, 2008, pp. 77, 106